Sigyn: Our Lady of the Staying Power

SIGYN

OUR LADY OF THE STAYING POWER

A Devotional to the Norse Goddess of Constancy

GALINA KRASSKOVA

SANNGETALL PRESS

Sigyn: Our Lady of the Staying Power
Second Edition © 2020

First edition published 2009 by Asphodel Press

"Group Ritual to Honor Sigyn" originally appeared in *Feeding The Flame* © 2007 Galina Krasskova, Asphodel Press. All other works © 2009 their respective authors and used with permission.

Front Cover Art © Lynn Perkins
Back Cover Art © Grace Palmer
Interior Illustrations © Abby Helasdottir

All rights reserved. No part of this book may be reproduced in any form or by any means without the permission of the author.

This book is dedicated to Fuensanta Arismendi Plaza, the most devoted Sigyn's woman that I know, a woman who has served (all unbeknownst to her) as my spiritual director, my teacher, my inspiration. You make me a better person and you enable me to serve my Gods more fully, rightly, and well. Vielen Dank, meine liebe Mutti. Ich habe dich immer in meinem Herz.

"My love is my weight."

- St. Augustine

CONTENTS

Foreword to the Second Edition 1
Introduction 5
Honoring Sigyn: A Mini Book of Hours 21
Setting up an Altar to Sigyn 25
Making the Everyday Sacred 33
Prayer and the Simplicity of Gratitude 37
Sigyn Prayer Beads 43
Three Centering Prayers 49
For Sigyn 53
Daily Prayer 55
Evening Prayer 57
Rituals for Sigyn 59
An Evening Rite to Honor Sigyn 61
A Group Ritual to Honor Sigyn 65
Meditation: Learning to Listen 73
Twelve Virtues of Sigyn 75
A Meditation on Sigyn's Bowl 85
In Praise of Sigyn 89
Sigyn: Woman of Valor 91
Five for Sigyn 93
Incantation Fetter 95
Litany for Sigyn 97

Epilogue 99
Suggestions for Further Reading 101
About the Author 103

FOREWORD TO THE SECOND EDITION

I did not expect to write a second edition of this particular book. I love Sigyn now, if it is possible, even more than I did in 2009 when I first wrote the volume you now hold in your hands. So much has changed in my life though, including the death of my adopted mom, Fuensanta, in 2010. She was, in so many ways, a conduit to Sigyn for me, and a very holy woman. I was afraid of what I would find here with her gone, having moved to the realm of the ancestors. Loki introduced me to Sigyn but it was Mutti who brought me to Her truly, and the prayers and rituals here are touchstones, filled with magic, on the path of that devotion. I was almost afraid to touch them. I was afraid the magic would disappear, and I would find those devotional pathways barren and cold. Sometimes that happens, after all, and despite our best efforts; grief causes our hearts to harden. I prayed it would not be so here and my prayers were rewarded. When I read back through this small book, each word was as vibrant as when I initially wrote or collected them, and their magic I now give to you.

Sigyn is truly the Blessed Lady of Constancy and

Devotion. She knows grief and loss, but also joy and healing, and everything in between. Her love is as deeply rooted as the oldest, tallest, strongest mountain. It is a force that not even Odin Himself can sway. She can teach you how to keep the fire of devotion burning cleanly and brightly even in the darkest shadows of grief. She is made of grit and knows how to meet struggles with clear-eyed focus. This too, She can teach. And…how to sum up a Deity in a few paltry words? It is impossible.

Somehow it is bittersweet revisiting these old haunts. It's not that I haven't spent the intervening years in devotion to Sigyn, among the other Deities of my household. I have honored Her regularly. It's that I am so different from who I was when I wrote this book and it opens windows into the past, into places I was carried by a mother who loved me, who refused to let fear, pain, and grief drag me down. I know the tremendous and blessed magnitude of power that is this Goddess, and I know how deeply She may transform a life. She is Our Lady of the Staying Power, and will stay the course to the end of our journey and beyond, if we open our hearts to Her. There is nothing more that I can say about Her. I invite You to fall into devotion to Her yourselves.

On a practical note, there are a few changes from the first edition to this one. I have removed several pieces because I have fallen out of contact with the authors and did not want to presume their renewed permission to publish. I have also added several prayers that I have written in the past two years.

May Sigyn bless your endeavors, and may this book bring you closer to Her in devotion.

GALINA KRASSKOVA
BEACON, NY
MAY 15, 2020

INTRODUCTION

This is not a book of lore. It could not be, even if that was what I intended. There simply aren't enough surviving references in the lore to flesh out a devotional to Sigyn. She is not alone in sharing this predicament. The same can be said of many of our Goddesses. For those who share a love for these Deities, however, this is hardly a reason to limit one's devotional practices. It means instead that we must listen with our hearts, what Sufi mystic and poet Rumi called "the ear in the center of the chest." Here we must put the lore aside and work instead from longing, a deep longing and hunger to touch and be touched by our Gods. That can be a task fraught with terror, for with it comes an immense vulnerability. Sigyn is all about that holy vulnerability, vulnerability and an earth-shattering love that defies all boundaries, all opposition, and all anguish.

    I've written extensively both in my articles and my various books about the importance of developing what I call "devotional consciousness." To my mind this is the most basic and most important of spiritual tools. It's the foundation on which everything else we will ever do for our Gods rests. Prayer (both spontaneous and formulaic), meditation, rituals, and offerings are the building blocks of a strong and resilient spirituality, one that can bring the devotee closer to the Gods, one that can enhance daily life, one that can bring immense joy. One of the goals of this type of work is to create a mental, emotional, and spiritual attitude of receptivity to the Gods.

I don't think that such devotional consciousness is the purview of mystics or shamans or "holy" people only. In fact, I think it's something that every single person can aspire to, each in his or her own way. For some, that may mean developing a daily prayer practice. For others, it may mean touching the Gods most while engaged in diapering a child, planting a vegetable garden, doing one's finances, or cleaning one's house. There are hundreds of ways — to again quote Rumi — to kneel and kiss the ground. The important thing, to my mind at least, is that we endeavor to do so in some special way. Developing that individual practice, whatever it may be, centering one's heart in some small way around the Gods, making them the North Star, the compass by which our lives are guided is the most important thing a person can do; it's the foundation for any truly resilient spirituality. Spirituality is the inner world Tree that in turn sustains our lives.

Nor are these practices something stolen from Christianity, as I have often heard Heathens assert. Oh, they can be Christian, and certainly Christianity took these practices and ran with them throughout their two-thousand-year history, but they can just as easily be Polytheist, Pagan, or Heathen, or Muslim, or Jewish, etc.

INTRODUCTION

Historically, we find the concept of devotion embedded in nearly every faith the world over. For those who think that prayer is something only monotheists engage in, consider this: the earliest known prayers in the world were written by a woman, a priestess of the Gods Nanna and Inanna, in ancient Sumer. That is about as Polytheist as one can get. Denying ourselves such powerful spiritual tools as prayer, meditation, ritual and devotional practice because Christians also use them is shortsighted in the extreme. It gives to monotheism a power that it does not and should not possess, power over our own spirituality. Instead, I say learn from the ways in which various faiths have developed these practices. Learn from them and make these practices your own. We don't know what our ancestors did. We have no written records. I speculate this is because ancient Heathen religions developed in what was primarily an oral culture. Literacy did not become the primary mode of record keeping until Christianity had already become the dominant religion in the North. This is a tremendously important fact. What we have left, what Heathenry refers to as its lore, is but a drop in the ocean of what must have once been a vast storehouse of prayers, stories, and sacred rites. So we are left with a choice: we can choose to believe that our ancestors had no concept of the sacred, no concept of mystery, no concept of what religious scholar Rudolf Otto calls the numinous *tremendum et fascinans*; or we can choose to believe that they did in fact not only understand these concepts but have a deeply reverent way of interacting with the Holy Powers. The choice seems simple.

I belong to Odin and that colors everything in my life, most especially my devotional practices. Odin is a God of extremes. What He can ask of His devotees can be a terrifying manifestation of that reality. Sigyn is different, though, and I often come to Her as to a sweet oasis in the deepest desert of my spiritual life. She is not about extremes at all. She is about constancy. Constancy is Her only extreme: constancy of love, constancy of purpose, constancy of effort. Those self-same things lie at the heart of devotional practice. There's no secret to great success here, there is only constancy of effort. Perhaps that is one of the reasons Sigyn's name means "Victory Woman." She is the hidden flame in the center of a heart on fire with purpose and love for the Gods. She is the hearthkeeper of that flame, and its most ardent tender.

I love Sigyn dearly. She is the one Goddess to Whom I feel most strongly connected. I consider my connection to Her, being opened to Her presence, one of the greatest spiritual gifts I have ever been given. In part because of Sigyn, I have been made rich in blessings. A Sigyn's woman has been one of my most important teachers, instilling in me greater mindfulness, greater humility before the Gods, and greater compassion within the community — all difficult lessons for a headstrong Odin's woman to learn. She, like the Goddess she serves, has challenged me again and again to set aside my fear of my own gentleness, my own vulnerability, my own heart. She, like Sigyn, has challenged me to accept and recognize these things as equally valuable gifts as those the War God I serve may bring. For one whose feet tread so surely the warrior's path, that is not easy. That is, however, exactly one of the lessons Sigyn teaches. It is what She Herself does best and by doing so She sustains all She loves and holds dear.

Because there are so very few references made about Her in the surviving lore, because Her nature (as those of us who honor Her have experienced it) is quiet and unassuming, and because She is the wife of Loki, the most controversial of Norse Deities, I have found that She is often marginalized or ignored in the modern Northern Tradition, with very few exceptions. As the issue of whether or not to honor Jotun Deities becomes a majorly contested site within modern Heathenry, inflaming hostilities and emotions on both sides of the debate, Her worship falls ever more so into the shadow of ideology and iconoclasm. It is as though She is guilty by association, as the saying goes — as if we in our hubris dare ascribe human guilt to a God.

I believe that Sigyn Herself, and Her story as it has come down to us in the surviving lore, has much to teach modern Northern Traditionalists, particularly as we do tend to be a contentious group of denominations. She is one of the Asynjur, the Goddesses of the Aesir, wed to a Jotun. Her marriage itself is a site of grievous political conflict, for the two tribes were and are often at war. Ours is not a peaceful religion. Struggle, contention, conflict of opposites are embedded in our very cosmology, in the very story of our origins wherein ice and fire fought for dominance and created life out of the power of their struggle. Sigyn can teach us to rise above such partisan conflicts be they large or small, to see the humanity, the individuality, the integrity of the other side. Because She "fits" nowhere, no one is "other" to Her. Because She has been cast out, She knows the true blessing of hospitality, the generosity of heart that goes well beyond tribe, reputation, or appearances. Because She has lost everything: home, stability, children, husband — for could Loki ever be the same after Their ordeal in the cave? — She understands grief and the cost of hatred. She knows how to rebuild, restore, and nourish a home within Herself. It is to Sigyn then that we can and perhaps should turn within our communities. She knows how to pick up the pieces after devastation, but how much better to call upon Her wisdom before that point occurs?

I believe the Northern Tradition communities are terrified of devotion, of what that means for themselves, and what that means about the Gods Themselves. I believe there is immense hostility toward devotional work in part because it lifts the focus off the safety net of lore and casts it solidly into the realm of personal experience, or gnosis if you will, and personal experience can be messy. It may contain contradictions. It may go beyond what a community is comfortable with. It may arouse fear, anger, hatred, or intense devotion. It's not safe. I believe that lore, so useful in contextualizing religious practice has instead become a fetter through overly rigid and literal interpretation, interprettation that lacks either inspiration or actual love for the Gods Themselves; and on every side of the debate there is anger. So now I say, why? Who are we doing this for? Rather than expending energy, time, and emotion in spewing vitriol back and forth at each other, isn't that better spent in loving and honoring the Gods? One thing that I have learned above all else from Sigyn: priorities. What is your priority: loving and honoring the Gods or creating divisive conflict? There are a thousand ways to kneel and kiss the ground.[1]

I am not a peaceful person. I am usually the first one ready to dive headlong into any conflict that I care passionately about. It's taken me many years to learn to appreciate the alternate strategy that Sigyn can teach. Sigyn's way takes such courage. Her way is a quiet way of personal mindfulness and dedication. It is a simple way. It is a terrifying way. Walking in Her footsteps means that there is no place to hide: no fine words, no angry posturing, no pride, no ego, no boasting — Her deeds are boast enough. There is nothing but what must be done, and a heart committed to the doing. Sigyn's way is simple: constancy of the heart, in the face of hatred, opposition, jealousy, slander, exhaustion, grief, anguish, rage, despair and a thousand other obstacles that life has a way of creating. She is constancy of purpose. My beloved friend, spiritual mother, and teacher Fuensanta Arismendi calls Sigyn "My Lady of the Staying Power," because She is vast, and Her strength is vast even as it is so completely unassuming. It simply is and will not be moved. She is the "Lady of

---

[1] Barks, Coleman, (2003). *Rumi: The Book of Love*. NY: Harper Collins Publishers, p. 123.

Unyielding Gentleness," for much the same reason. Her gentleness of spirit is Her shield and Her strength, and in it She is fierce. Her devotion is Her armor.

So, I offer this devotional to Her, because I love Her, because She has nurtured me, because I have learned so much from Her example, however imperfect my attempts to follow it, and because She has opened my heart in ways I never thought possible. Most of all, I offer this to Her because She is worthy of devotion. She brings victory as Her name implies: victory over the unruly passions of the heart, victory over our own base impulses, our selfishness, our fear, our pain, our longing. She brings us victory over ourselves. That is only one of the many gifts She holds out to those with the humility to seek Her out, this wise and gentle Goddess. In Her own way, She is as unyielding as Odin. She is at once merciful and implacable. May She be hailed. May She be honored, and may offerings be poured out before Her.

Hail Sigyn, wife of Loki.
Hail Sigyn, Mother of Narvi and Vali.
Hail Sigyn, of the unconquerable heart.
Hail Sigyn, of the Staying Power.
Hail Sigyn, Victory Woman.
May You ever be praised!

GALINA KRASSKOVA
NEW YORK CITY
FEBRUARY 2, 2009

SIGYN

Sigyn is mentioned a mere handful of times in the surviving lore. References to Her may be found in the *Voluspa*, the *Lokasenna*, the *Gylfaginning*, and the *Skaldskaparmal* and *Þórsdrápa*. What we actually learn from these references is regrettably little:

- Sigyn is Loki's wife.
- She is listed amongst the Asynjur, the Goddesses of the Aesir.
- She is the mother, by Loki, of Narvi and Vali. When Loki was bound in the cave as punishment for His role in Baldur's death, Vali was turned into a wolf. He then killed His brother by tearing Him apart. Narvi's intestines were used as part of the binding securing Loki.
- Sigyn, ostensibly having witnessed all of this, stayed by Loki during His punishment, holding a bowl over His face to catch the poison that dripped from a serpent the Goddess Skadhi had secured above His head. For this reason, Loki is sometimes referred to as the "Burden of Sigyn's Arms."
- Sigyn's name means "victory woman."

Nothing else survives that may point to the ways in which Her nature and roles were conceived of by pre-Christian Heathens. Nothing survives of Her worship. This may be viewed as a great loss, or it may be viewed as a great opportunity for we have the chance to start anew, going directly to this Goddess to learn how She wants to be honored today.

In my own experience of Sigyn, and that of the handful of Sigyn's people that I know, She seems to often reveal Herself in one of two ways: either as a delightfully child-like young girl or, conversely, as a wife: implacable, resilient, post the ordeal of the cave, burdened by the overwhelming grief of the loss of Her children. Either way, Her presence is compelling and immense. She is the only Goddess I have ever encountered who evokes in me a feeling of protectiveness. Perhaps this is simply because when Loki first "introduced" me to Her, it was in Her child aspect that She came. I have written about Her before, both in *Exploring the Northern Tradition* and *Feeding the Flame*, the latter of which is a devotional to Loki and His family. It is not my desire to repeat myself unduly here. Suffice it to say, that Sigyn is a complex Goddess with a great deal to teach, and while She may very often choose to reveal Herself in the ways noted above, one should not think that She is in any way limited to those two roles. It is up to every devotee to discover Her for themselves, to pave the road through devotion by which She can touch their hearts.

Taken from lore, Sigyn has one primary mystery: She endured. She consciously chose to honor the commitments of Her heart and to endure in the face of unprecedented loss, grief, and misery. Loki's ordeal in the cave, perhaps the defining moment of His mythos, was also *Her* ordeal in the cave. The difference is that She consciously chose to endure it. Over the years, I have encountered many discussions in various online Heathen and Asatru forums in which Sigyn was dismissed as little more than the epitome of the abused wife. Moderns all too often seem to read into Her story passivity, victimhood, and a regrettable lack of agency. I truly do not know whether this is because She demonstrated these arguably most Heathen of virtues in defense of Loki, who is a very controversial figure in the modern community, because we know nothing else of Her story via the lore, or because She isn't depicted as bold, brash, or sexually independent (like Freya). I would hate to think that Her strength, Her loyalty, Her constancy are all too often overlooked perhaps because these things are exercised primarily in the enclosure of Her domestic sphere.

It seems to me as though Sigyn's world was defined by love: love of Her husband, love of Her children, love of Her family as a whole. Given that Loki's other wife is Angurboda, the mighty chieftainess of the Ironwood, are we really to believe that He would choose a doormat as a mate? It makes far more sense to me (and, granted, this comes in part from my personal experience of Sigyn) to wonder at the quiet strength that must have provided a soothing haven to this most quixotic and fiery of Gods. It is a mistake to view Her gentleness as weakness. Because She is never seen external to Her home and family does not mean that She is powerless. What it means is that She created *inangard*, the sacred enclosure of the home, for a God who was otherwise rootless. She rooted Him, balanced Him, accepted Him, and above all loved Him. It was Her choice to do this. Herein lies the conundrum of modernity: when we accept that women have free agency, we must also acknowledge that sometimes that agency will be exercised consciously and freely in ways we might disagree with. I cannot help but speculate on whether or not Sigyn is so easily dismissed because She was, essentially, the quintessential *Hausfrau*, and this is a role that in today's world, is also all too often devalued.

Several years ago, a Christian friend, a priest, observing the less than pleasant dynamic that so often characterizes Heathen community discussions and debate turned to me and asked, apologetically, "Where is love in your faith? Where is compassion?" At the time, I merely responded that it is in the lessons the Gods teach us directly, not the lore, unless it be hidden within the dictates on hospitality. As I myself have grown in my faith (hopefully) and as I have grown closer to Sigyn (definitely), I've discovered the answer to my friend's question: Sigyn. Sigyn embodies and teaches everything we could ever hope to learn about love, compassion and many other virtues as well. Where is love in our religion? It rests with Sigyn. Where is compassion? In Her heart. Perhaps by casting Her and by extension Her family out of our devotions, we're turning a blind eye to those things as well.

Sigyn's story is also one of victory: victory over wrenching circumstances, over pain, loss, despair, and anguish. She chooses to endure and by doing so, She triumphs. As Fuensanta Arismendi, an ardent Sigyn's woman, once said: Sigyn's strength is in Her heart. Her heart is invincible.

Despite the fact that there is a dearth of information in the lore on Sigyn, She has a small collection of sacred by-names, or *heiti*. Known *heiti* for Her, taken both from lore and modern practice include:

- Wife of Loki
- Incantation-Fetter (*Þórsdrápa*)[2]

---

[2] This is a particularly fascinating by-name in what it implies: that She has the ability to bind and ward off magical incantations. Among possible interpretations, this could be seen in Her act of warding Loki from the magical binding and torture inflicted on Him by the Aesir, or it could be a reference to Her ability to make sacred the holy inangard of the home. As Loki's devotee Mordant Carnival noted, "Then there's that tantalizing kenning for Sigyn: *galdrs hapt* or 'Incantation-fetter' (according to Faulkes' translation of the *Þórsdrápa*, where we find the Loki-kenning *farmr arma galdrs hapts*. Some have suggested that *galdrs hapts* refers to Gullveig, but since Loki is nowhere else kenned as Gullveig's lover Sigyn is the more rational choice).

"Why is She being referred to as Incantation-Fetter? This, to me, implies some story that hasn't come down to us, perhaps one in which Sigyn displays the ability to thwart magical charms. (I can't help thinking of the *Runatál* section of *Hávamál*, which makes reference to charms both for binding one's enemies and for freeing oneself from fetters.)

"As a side note, the name Narvi crops up elsewhere in lore. It's given as the name of a Jotun, the father of Nótt

- Lady of the Staying Power
- Lady of Unyielding Gentleness
- Lady of the Unconquerable Heart
- Mother of Narvi and Vali
- North Star
- Victory Woman

Every time I hear the kenning for Loki "Burden of Sigyn's arms," it brings to mind Michelangelo's pietá, not the one in Rome but the one in the Uffizi in Florence which shows Mary, Joseph, and the Magdalene holding a Christ made doubly heavy by the burden of a dead body and by the burden of grief. Here Michelangelo caught something essential about the nature of grief: it has a terrible weight. Shakespeare said in King John, where he has a queen sit down on the floor next to the throne having lost a son (and Sigyn is a queen), "…for my grief is so great that none but the huge firm earth can bear it." That to me, is Sigyn. She bears the unbearable. There's no glamour in Her ordeal.

With ordeals like Odin's, it's nine days and then it's over. It's the plucking of an eye and then it's over. I mean no disrespect, but Sigyn didn't know when or even if Her ordeal would ever be

---

(Night). It is unclear whether They're the same individual; perhaps there were two Narvis? If they were, though, that would make Sigyn the grandmother of Night, a very potent role."

over. Not to mention no mother ever gets over the ordeal of losing a child, something Odin also understood. But there is no glamour: you do what's right, and you do it again and again and again, and that's very unpopular. There's no glamour, no sweeping gestures, and no one to sing your praises. The heart is a terrible thing.
- Fuensanta Arismendi

Finally, as both a Goddess and a woman, Sigyn has immense dignity. This is something that is rarely touched upon even by those who honor Her regularly: She has an enormous amount of dignity. She never complains. She never explains. She never blames. She never shows off or emphasizes the pain and difficulty of what She does. She never seeks attention. She just does what needs to be done and allows Her deeds to speak for themselves. There is something remarkably noble in Her attitude. She simply does not stoop to complain. There's tremendous dignity in that.

Of all the Nine Worlds, Helheim was unjustly the richer because it held Her son.
- Fuensanta Arismendi

HONORING SIGYN
A MINI BOOK OF HOURS

Devotional practice is the art of religious love.
- Silence Maestas[3]

There are many, many ways to engage in devotional practice. What ties the various techniques such as ritual, prayer, meditation, and study together is that when engaged in regularly, they have the power to dramatically enhance one's spiritual practices. These things help to discipline the mind and heart to the Gods, to create the necessary emotional and spiritual receptivity which can nurture and nourish spiritual life. Devotional practices are grounded in a certain interiority of practice and it is from this interior journey that one is able to establish the building blocks of true piety.

Piety is a word that has fallen out of favor in modern religious circles. Derived from the Latin *pietas*, it literally means dutiful conduct, especially toward the Gods. It encompasses a broad spectrum of right

---

[3] Maestas, Silence, (2008). *Walking the Heartroad.* MA: Asphodel Press, p. i.

relationship and right action: toward oneself, toward one's fellow humans, one's ancestors, and, of course, toward the Gods. It implies a way of being in the world, and a way of mindful interaction. Essentially, piety is the thorough, all-encompassing expression of ongoing and evolving devotion. At its best, it is quiet and forthright. True piety does not rest in broad, conspicuous gestures or flamboyant, seemingly "religious" behavior. Such things would be caricatures of this virtue. Rather, real piety lies in making one's heart open to the Gods and striving every hour of every day, as best we can to allow that awareness to govern our every deed. And we do this knowing that in our imperfection we shall fail, we shall have setbacks, and we shall have to get up, retrace our steps, and forge onward again and again and again. Piety involves the grace on ongoing perseverance. It is this virtue that both informs and flows from ongoing devotional practice. With Sigyn, it is often held forth in very practical ways.

The remainder of this book explores the basics of devotional work centered around Sigyn. There are prayers, rituals, and meditations all designed to bring the reader into greater concert with this Goddess. The material presented here is merely a guideline for those taking their first steps in devotional work — and it is work. Simply building the daily habit of turning one's mind consciously toward the Gods can be an extremely difficult process to internalize. Sometimes even knowing where to begin can be a struggle. The prayers, meditations, and rituals given here provide a basic map to a rich, endless, and extraordinary territory. How far one goes depends upon each individual him or herself. All I know is that the journey is well worth the effort.

SETTING UP AN ALTAR TO SIGYN

Anyone who has read any of my other works knows that I set great store in altar work. I have found no better way for introducing someone to specific Deities, for expressing in passionate symbolism that the Gods have a place in one's life, for beginning the process of engaging in committed devotional practice than by setting up an altar. It's something that appeals to one's entire sensorium. The altar becomes a living representation of one's ongoing dialogue with the Gods. It's a visible reminder of the spiritual reciprocity that one hopes to encourage by devotional practice. Therefore, it should come as no surprise that the first step that I am going to recommend, in learning to honor Sigyn, is that of setting up a household altar to Her.

In many ways, maintaining a small household altar or shrine to Her is particularly appropriate as She is a Goddess of domesticity and simplicity. One of Sigyn's graces is the ability to find the sacred in the everyday. She is very much a Goddess of mindfulness, and of infusing the ordinary with the sacred. I keep Her altar in my bedroom, because it's the prettiest room in my home, but the kitchen would be just as appropriate a place, given that it is considered, in many traditions, to be the heart of the home. Wherever you choose to create your altar to Her, the important thing is that it remain in use. An altar should never grow stagnant. It should never be allowed to collect dust. The altar should serve as a very well-trod pathway between you and the God or Goddess you're choosing to honor by its construction.

Altars are very simple to create. The only necessary warning is that they tend to grow and take over any flat space in one's home! I've seen altars created on windowsills, bookcases, tabletops, shelves. I've seen them made in boxes (including, in one case, an Altoids tin), in drawers, and in books that could then be carried. The creation of an altar is limited only by one's own creative inspiration. There is no right or wrong way to do this so long as one is guided by devotion, love, and respect.

The first step is to choose a space. Where is your altar going to be placed? Once you've selected a workable spot, decide what you're going to put on your altar. Think about what reminds you of Sigyn, what She might like, what speaks to you of the relationship you're seeking to create. Sadly, there are very few images and statues on the market of the lesser venerated Gods and Goddesses but, if you are very lucky, or if you are an artist or craftsperson yourself, finding and/or creating an image of Sigyn may be a powerful meditation and point of connection in and of itself. If you have the skills to create an image, this provides a powerful opportunity not only to make a lovely offering to Her, but to consciously choose the first aspect of Her nature that you wish to approach. Will your image be of the Sigyn as a child, as a young woman, Loki's bride, a loving mother, an anguished wife, loyal in the cave, unyielding in Her support of Her husband? How will you choose to depict Her? Art of all types is a powerful medium through which the Gods can work through us and through which we can connect to the Gods. If you don't have the ability to craft your own image, don't worry. It's not necessary to have one. One day I hope to see a myriad of images of all of our Gods and Goddesses easily available online, but that day has not yet come.

Once you have chosen what to place on your altar, do so knowing that you can change and adapt it as your relationship with Her grows. There really is no right or wrong way to work this process. Devotional work is very much an individual process, unique to each and every person even when the same prayers are being said, and the same devotional actions being taken.

I can offer some suggestions as to what to put on Her altar, but this is based on my own experience of Sigyn, and should not in any way serve to limit one's own altar construction. The following suggestions are not in any way based on lore (save for the symbolism of the bowl) but are drawn from my own and other people's personal gnosis.

- **Symbols:** old-fashioned keys, bowl or cup, heart, star

- **Sigyn as the child:** pink, lavender, or blue altar cloths, pretty dolls, stuffed animals, flowers, childlike things, lady bugs[4], beads.

- **Sigyn as the mourning wife and mother:** grey or dark brown cloths, wooden or metal bowl, ashes. I have known several Sigyn's women who associated the doe with Her.

- **Herbs:** flowers, especially violets, daisies, chamomile, and thistles. I often given Her roses, especially ones in colors like blush pink that I associate with Her. I don't think any flower would be inappropriate though for this Goddess.

- **Rune:** Nauthiz, some Sigyn's women see Berkana with Her.

- **Stones I associate with Her:** rose quartz, green garnet, pearls (I personally do not buy pearls because the way they are harvested is often harmful to the ocean. This is a taboo placed on me as a result of my devotion to Ran, Aegir, and Their Nine Daughters. An exception to this would be the purchase of estate pearls[5]. Still, all this being said, I do strongly associate pearls with Sigyn perhaps because they are traditionally associated with mourning).

---

[4] Traditionally believed to bring luck, ladybugs are also fierce predators and will keep a garden free of other pests like aphids and cabbage bugs. They're little warrior bugs.

[5] Pearls from pre-1950 were not harvested using modern methods.

SETTING UP AN ALTAR TO SIGYN

- **Food Offerings:** sweets, cakes, cookies, chocolate for Her as child, bread, macaroni and cheese (at least one Sigyn's woman swears She likes this), butter, sweet wines.

- **Other offerings:** honor Narvi and Vali, put something to represent them on the altar (perhaps toys as They were Her children), mourn for Her children, hold the bowl (see meditation below), help children in need, donate to organizations that help mothers and/or children in need, feed the hungry/donate time or money to organizations that feed the hungry, donate to war relief organizations or organizations that help refugees, particularly women and children, commit to regular prayer practice honoring Her. Be loyal to whatever you love when you feel you do not have the strength to do so and offer that to Sigyn. When it's no effort, it's just you but when you feel you cannot do this any longer, that is the effort that can be given to Sigyn.

- **Things not to do:** insult Loki, insult or demean Her children, ignore Her children.

Do not think that because Sigyn is gentle, She cannot get angry. Her gentleness is choice, not weakness. It is an inexorable choice. She is every bit as unyielding as any other Deity in Heathen lore. You cannot force Sigyn ever to depart from the chosen path of Her heart. If that includes smiting someone, She'll do it, but not as a reaction. She is above reaction. She does not react unthinkingly. She chooses consciously and in the fullness of Her power.

Early in 2008, a fellow spirit-worker (who also happens to be a Voudoun priest) told me of attending a ritual held by a group of Heathens in, I believe, New Jersey. I myself was not present, so the story that I am about to relay is based on what my colleague later told me. The blót was in honor of Sigyn. At first, I was very happy to hear that others within the Northern Tradition community were beginning to openly honor Her. My friend just smiled and cautioned me to wait. There was more to her tale. Apparently, after the ritual, but before folks had been dispersed (i.e., while still in the enclosure of sacred space) a woman present had begun vociferously slandering Loki (and by extension Sigyn). Sigyn loves Her husband very much. My friend, coming as she does from Voudoun, could not at first believe that someone would have the hubris and audacity, not to mention complete lack of courtesy, hospitality, manners, and survival instinct, to stand in sacred space and verbally harangue a Deity so closely related to the Deity being honored in the recent ritual. Within moments of having uttered her unthinking words slandering Sigyn's husband, the woman in question got hit with a sudden cluster migraine so severe that she had to be removed from the ritual and taken home. Neither my friend nor I find this coincidental. Our ancestors certainly knew better than to slander the Gods in such a fashion. We'd best learn that lesson too. One simply does not stand in sacred space and utter words of hate about those that this Goddess loves. She tends to get a bit peeved. As a

SETTING UP AN ALTAR TO SIGYN

Sigyn's woman that I know commented upon hearing this story: the slanderous woman is fortunate she didn't get explosive diarrhea. It would have been fitting. So, be respectful, just as you would with any other Deity. Sigyn is not the lesser because She chooses not to flaunt Her power.

> Above all else, keep it simple. Sigyn is not about the ornate.
>
> - Fuensanta Arismendi

MAKING THE EVERYDAY SACRED

> It's like having a baby. Loving the baby is all very well but that love is expressed by cleaning and caring for the baby: by changing its diapers, by keeping its ass clean, by feeding and burping it. Love is not some abstract thing. Love rolls up its sleeves and gets to work.
> - Fuensanta Arismendi

One of Sigyn's many graces is the ability to imbue even the most mundane task with elements of the sacred. She sees the holy in everything. Every act She takes, no matter how simple, flows from the love She bears. Every act is a prayer in motion. For those that honor Her, and even more so for those that belong to Her, embodying Her wisdom rarely means undergoing painful physical ordeals (like Odin sometimes demands), or being at the center of a group or organization (as Frigga's people often excel at). Sigyn's way is that of simplicity and mindfulness. She diligently cares for the simplest of tasks out of love and joy in the work itself. In some respects, Sigyn has a lot in common with Frau

Hölle. They both do what needs to be done, even when it isn't at all glamorous. They're both Goddesses of sacred industry.

We often read "fairy tales" in an entirely unjustified spirit of smugness. "Hah!" we snort. "Didn't that stupid girl know she'd come to a bad end if she didn't take the bread out of the oven? *I* would have taken it out!" So why are we ignoring the piles of paperwork on the desk? "You'd think she would have had the sense to pick those apples!" we sneer. So why is the bathtub dirty? How often do we incur Frau Hölle's displeasure? How often do we deserve Her praise? The same might be said of Sigyn. One of the most undervalued and underexplored ways of honoring Her, is to infuse everyday work, the mundanity of everyday life with an awareness of love, respect (for the task at hand), and the sacred. There is immense sacredness in creating order.

In that old-fashioned haven, "a well-ordered house," life has some degree of serenity: time is not wasted in looking for objects, the eye is not distracted by chaos, many decisions are made once and for all. That dreaded concept, routine, is really that which frees us for other things. Clutter, trash, and dirt are traps for the energy that should flow through our home and our lives. Our homes are our sacred space, an extension of our altars. Just how do you treat your sacred space?

> Hold the space against entropy, dirt, neglect, against passivity. In all four corners you have, you hold the space. Upward and downward, you hold

the space against chaos. When you clean, you invoke order and purity, and guard sacred space against its opposite. This is what I do every day when I clean the toilet. It's what I do.

- Fuensanta Arismendi

Every piece of clothing on the floor is a deferred decision, a refusal to pick the apples. Every bill that is tossed on the table with an "I can't be bothered with this now," is a refusal to take the bread out of the oven. Every time we buy an object because we cannot find that object in the chaos of our household, or because we hoard so many items we have forgotten we own it, we disregard both Sigyn and Frau Hölle's teachings. Choosing to live mindfully, to embrace simplicity and a paring down of excess is a powerful way to open the door to Sigyn's blessings. Remember, the most powerful act that Sigyn is known, in lore, for doing — holding the bowl above Loki's face to capture poison — was done with an everyday household implement. That is where Her power lies: in using everyday things with extraordinary commitment.

My Lady of everyday virtues, please help me remember
to execute each task in its time, not my own.
May I learn that bread must be taken out of the oven
when it is baked, not when I feel like it.
May I learn that apples must be picked
when they are ripe, not when "I'll get around to it."
May I perform everyday tasks mindfully,
knowing that tasks dictate the doing,

and the time and fashion of the doing.
May my work be blessed by performing it
in the proper spirit.
For only then will I too be blessed by my work.

PRAYER AND THE SIMPLICITY OF GRATITUDE

> God gives his gifts where he finds the vessel empty enough to receive them.
> - C. S. Lewis

Prayer is one of the most important tools in developing a strong spiritual practice. It is a way of communicating with the Gods, of nourishing one's relationship with Them. It can also be a powerful lifeline at times of struggle and pain. Bracketing one's day with regular intervals of prayer helps the devotee remain mindful of the Gods and our connection to Them. It can also help us to see Their presence in our world. There are few greater spiritual gifts than learning how to pray with passionate engagement. I know that in the Northern Tradition community, prayer is often dismissed as groveling submission. Sadly, in many cases, this incredibly powerful tool may have been ruined for some people by upbringings in which prayer was misused as a weapon. Reclaiming its integrity of purpose can be the most difficult challenge one ever engages upon. It's well worth it though. This is too powerful and useful a gift in the richness of our spiritual lives to dismiss. It's too beautiful a blessing to sacrifice on the altar of fear, or spiritual indolence. It's too important a tool for us to allow it to be stolen out of our lives.

Prayer is not about asking for things. It's about developing a fluid, resilient, reciprocal relationship with Beings that we love, respect, and honor. It's about expressing gratitude for who we are and those gifts we've been given. I think that there's an unfortunate attitude not just within the Northern Tradition, but within modern religion as a whole, of focusing on prayer as a means of petitioning the Gods. Yes, the Gods are givers of all good things. Yes, prayer is a needful activity. That doesn't mean, however, that we should harass the Gods as though it was their obligation to answer our every summons. Rather prayer is a tool by which we can enter into passionate engagement with our Gods. It is a means of befriending Them, of accepting our place as Their children, Their younger kin, Their devotees. Hand in hand with prayer, it can be very helpful to develop a gratitude practice.

There are times in everyone's life when we wonder if what we do is worth it. There are times, where the frustration, exhaustion, and constant work threaten to overwhelm us. There are times, many of them, when burn-out threatens; and there are times when we wish for nothing more than a normal, uneventful life one that doesn't involve dealing with Gods. There's no shame in any of this; it happens. It's part of being human. There are also times, however, beautiful, magical, breathtaking moments where the Gods send us the immense gift of showing us exactly how much They love us. It's all a matter of opening our eyes and learning to be mindful of those small blessings. Those moments can make all the pain, frustration, and exhaustion worthwhile. They are small gifts of grace and more precious than any jewel. Sigyn with Her way of gentle simplicity can teach us to be aware of those blessings. One of the gifts that She brings is that of gratitude, for every single good thing in our lives, no matter how small.

Gratitude enhances our practice. It, like prayer, helps us hold the line when everything in our hearts and minds and very tired spirits says, "just give up." I have said it before and I will say it again: if you do the work, the Gods will provide. Recognizing that and allowing your heart to be filled with gratitude for that care, for that love, for those most unexpected of blessings, well, that's part of our work too and it's the part that can benefit us the most. Gratitude is about learning to see the magic in our lives, learning to see the ways in which we are surrounded every minute of every day by the blessings of the Gods.

We are not born knowing how to do this. The sensibilities of gratitude and prayer consciousness must be carefully cultivated as part of our devotion to our Gods. It takes care, time, and hard work. It takes commitment. That doesn't mean that it can't be a joyful process, but it's just that: a process. There are times where we can become very discouraged in our spiritual practices. There are times where it can seem pointless.

There are times when we can hit a spiritual plateau that seems unending. The important thing is to persevere.

Learning how to pray can be fraught with confusion and in truth, there are many ways to go about this. Action can be the most potent prayer of all, after all, especially where Sigyn is concerned. For me, much of my prayer is an ongoing dialogue with the Gods throughout my day, lacking in the formality of traditional, "set" prayers. Yet for learning how to focus one's mind on the practice of prayer, those traditional prayers can be very, very helpful. In part, this is because they engage not just our minds and hearts, but our hands as well. Working through a string of prayer beads engages that most intimate aspect of the sensorium: touch. For those drawn to this type of prayer, it helps ground those prayers in our consciousness. We are embodied beings after all and the body too is a spiritual tool. It's our ultimate conduit between the world of spirit and the human world.

The past few years have seen a growing interest within Paganism in general and the Northern Tradition in particular in the use of prayer beads. For people struggling with what to say and how to say it, prayer beads can be, if you'll pardon the pun, a godsend. Now, I'm not going to debate the question of historical accuracy. I don't know whether our Northern European pre-Christian ancestors used prayers beads and frankly, I don't particularly care. The important thing, to my mind at least, is that they are effective tools here and now. Using prayer beads to begin exploring prayer can also serve a double duty: since we can't go to our local religious store to purchase a set of Sigyn oriented prayer beads, most of us have to resort to crafting our own. That process in and of itself can be turned into a power meditation on Her nature.

The primary objection that I have encountered when the subject of prayer beads arises is in the formality and lack of spontaneity involved in this type of praying. That need not be the case however, if the act of prayer is approached as a living, transformative practice, grounded in love and devotion.

> I believe there is nothing repetitive about praying the same words every day. We're a different person every day and so our prayer too is different. A prayer that is spoken daily acquires a lustre, a patina made of all the meanings we wove into it such as only time and repetition can give.
>
> I believe these prayers are of use to the Gods because they're charged with our emotions, with our life force if you will, and this feeds Them. The Gods have been ignored, have been hungry for a long time. Daily prayer means daily food to Them. The certainty that They will be prayed to and fed tomorrow, as They were prayed to and fed today.
> - Fuensanta Arismendi

Sometimes the problem is knowing what to say. For those who struggle with extemporaneous prayers, working with beads can be an especially good place to begin. The next section presents an example of Sigyn-oriented prayer beads. I also encourage those interested in this type of prayer to consider creating your own unique set of beads for Sigyn. The possibilities are limitless.

SIGYN PRAYER BEADS

This set of beads begins with a tail of one key[6], one large bead, one ladybug bead, and another large bead. They then continue with a circlet comprised of three sets of one ladybug bead followed by three smaller beads[7]. The beads are separated by two small spacers between each bead and its successor.

The smaller beads involve hailing Her under specific by-names. As you do so, pause and meditate for a time on what each means. When She is hailed as "Victory Woman," for instance, don't just go onto the next bead. Take a few moments to really think about and picture Her ordeal in the cave, what it meant for Her to hold the bowl unwaveringly, what it meant for protection from poison to be Her universe for that time.

---

[6] A key is something many Sigyn's women associate with Her as Goddess of the home. In Norse and Viking Age cultures, keys were symbols of a woman's power. Upon marriage, men turned over the keys to their home, larder, and financial resources to their wives. Failing to do so, in some places, could result in immediate divorce. Many of our Goddesses, including, Frigga and Freya, may bear keys as a symbol of this type of domestic power and influence.

[7] You may add as many small beads as you wish, with each bead representing a different one of her praise names.

Think about what She must have gone through and try to open to that experience. Likewise, when thinking about Her name, "Incantation Fetter," spend a few moments contemplating on the reasons behind this particular name. Don't just rush through the beads. Try to internalize them and use each one as an opportunity to delve more deeply into Her sacred names, ancient and modern.)

Old-fashioned Key:
I begin with You, Sweet Sigyn, Lady of Loyalty, Delight of Loki's Hall.
I hail You always, Lady of unyielding gentleness, Lady of the staying power; not to what I think You are, but to what You know Yourself to be.

Big bead:
My Lord and my Lady, Loki and Sigyn, my Beloved Ones,
May Your voice always be heard by those You call to You.
May I love You always, beyond trust and mistrust.
May my surrender be complete and voluntary.
Give me this day the grace of Your presence.
When I fail You, of Your kindness, permit me to make amends.
Use me and teach me according to Your will.
And deliver me from all complacency.[8]

---

[8] Prayer by Fuensanta Arismendi.

Ladybug bead:
Be with me, Sigyn, that I may be mindful.
May I never take for granted that which nourishes my body.
May I never take for granted that which nourishes my soul.
Make me mindful, oh Goddess, that I may be constant, in a lifetime of devotions.
Because I love You, show me how to love You.

Big bead:
Repeat "My Lord and my Lady" prayer

Ladybug bead:
May my honor of You keep me mindful of my own duties.
Be always in my heart, oh Goddess.

Three small beads:
Hail to Sigyn, delight of Her husband.
Hail to Sigyn, devoted Mother.
Hail to Sigyn, who holds all things in Her heart.

Ladybug bead:
May my devotion to You never waver.
May You always be honored.

Three small beads:
Comforter of Loki, may You be comforted.
Shield of His heart, may You be strengthened.
Joy of His house and hall, may You be filled with joy.

Ladybug bead:
Gentle Goddess, may You find peace.
May your duty bring fruitful reward and surcease of sorrow to those You love.

Three small beads:
Hail to Sigyn, Lady of Unyielding Gentleness.
Hail to Sigyn, Lady of the Staying Power.
Hail to Sigyn, Victory Woman.

Ladybug bead:
May You find rest from the burden of Your sorrows.

Big bead:
Repeat "My Lord and my Lady" prayer

Ladybug bead:
Repeat Sigyn prayer.

Big bead:
Repeat "My Lord and my Lady" prayer

Key:
In all that I do, may I be mindful of Your example.
Hail, Sigyn.

This set of beads takes less than ten minutes to say and yet can serve as a powerful stepping stone to developing a greater relationship with Sigyn. I find that it's best not to try to memorize the individual prayers when working with beads, simply focus on saying them regularly and eventually sheer repetition will help you commit them to memory. (I have found that once they are memorized, though, the process of telling the beads changes yet again, becoming deeper and more organic.) Part of learning to pray is developing the habit, of gifting yourself with the discipline to commit a small amount of time each day. It need not be extensively time-consuming, but it needs to begin by building that ongoing habit of regular, centered mindfulness. Once that has been achieved, it's easy to move into informal, fluid prayer.

Even then, however, formal, "set" prayers have their place. They form a baseline of practice. Life can be difficult and sometimes, despite the best of intentions, it's all but impossible to achieve those moments of transcendent prayer that every devotee secretly hopes for. Sometimes it's all one can do to force oneself to sit down for ten minutes and even think about the Gods. It's at times like that where the prayer beads become an important spiritual touchstone. When you can do nothing else, you can do that.

THREE CENTERING PRAYERS

To Be Said Throughout the Day for Sigyn

Ordering one's day around the Gods via small but regular prayers can be a very potent means of developing devotional consciousness. Prayer of this sort need not be long. It is more a matter of turning one's mind and heart toward the Gods than of any verbal virtuosity. Sometimes one doesn't even need the words themselves. The following prayers[9] are short examples of the type of sacred utterance by which one may bracket one's day. I tend toward more formal prayers, but in truth, this type of centering prayer need be no more than the simple exhalation of Her name laden with all the emotion of one's heart.

Morning Prayer

With the rising of Sunna, I hail You,
Gentle Goddess, strong and wise.
Help me to be true to myself,

---

[9] Prayers by Galina Krasskova and Fuensanta Arismendi.

my Gods, and my commitments today.
Dear Sigyn, walk with me.
Be my shield, oh Goddess, be my strength.
Gift me with the grace of Your presence,
as I order my day through Your wisdom.

Afternoon Prayer

My Lady of Staying Power, my Beloved One,
You whose gentleness is vast as the sky,
Whose support is immense and silent as the earth,
Oh my North Star, My Lady of unyielding gentleness,
Teach me to sustain those I love.
Teach me to sustain You.

Evening Prayer

Oh my Adoration,
Loki's Sweet Adornment,
Treasure of His heart,
Blessing of His hearth,
Look upon me this night with grace,
Oh Goddess.
Thank You for this day
both in its boons
and its tangled unfolding.
May my lips always praise You
and my heart ever do You honor.
Hail, Sigyn.

Prayers need not be quite so formal either; at their best, they are spontaneous and passionate outpourings of devotion. Prayer is not just about supplication or seeking. It is about establishing a dialogue with the Gods and Goddesses that we love and respect. It's a way of communicating with Them and opening the doorway for Them to take active roles in our lives. Prayer is, in a word, essential.

FOR SIGYN

by Mordant Carnival

I adore You, my Lady.
You are sweet water washing wounds,
You are the gentle rain on parched earth,
You are spring flowers after the frost.
You are laughter welling up in the midst of sorrow, banishing it.
Your tender hand is laid on my brow,
You come to me like a breeze through a blossoming orchard.
Your breath is honeysuckle,
Your voice is music from a welcoming hall
At the end of a long journey.
You are the peace of my heart,
You are the ease of my sorrows.
Through the worst times,
The echo of Your strength sustains me;
When gladder times come,
Your joy makes mine more pure.
Oh Lady Sigyn, walk with me always;
Bright bride of Loki, let me stay by Your side.

DAILY PRAYER

by MM (age 6)

Make my heart your garden,
Till it faithfully, Lady Sigyn.
Because I love you,
Let me learn to love you better.
Hail, Sigyn.

EVENING PRAYER

by Anna Archer

Sigyn,
Make me a little voice within You, Lady.
Guide me to that place of stillness,
Where I may hear Your call.
Envelop me in Your protection.
Fill my heart with Your love,
That I may serve You always,
And well.

RITUALS FOR SIGYN

For some, structured rituals provide the best means of centering themselves around a specific Deity. Rituals can be a beautiful way of honoring a God or Goddess. They need not be long or formal (though they can be; I think the longest ritual I ever attended lasted roughly eight hours) — their power lies in their focus through repetitive or structured action.

A good ritual is like a well-written essay: it has a beginning, a middle, and an end, always coming back to one goal. First, one creates sacred space and moves oneself (or one's group) into that liminal place. This carries with it a certain receptivity of heart and mind, which in turns allows one to safely experience the numinous. Next, the main part of the ritual occurs: whatever actions, prayers, or activities are planned according to the purpose of the rite. Then, one should ground, center, offer thanks and close the ritual, transitioning back to mundane space.

Leading group rituals takes training and lots of practice but leading rituals for oneself need not involve quite so much structure. Much like altar making, a personal ritual can be as elaborate or as simple as each individual desires. The importance lies in how effective it is in helping one to draw closer to the Gods. Group rituals are fine and good but in the end, after all, the real spiritual work occurs alone.

AN EVENING RITE TO HONOR SIGYN

by M. Crawford

Take a few moments to center and ground yourself, letting the cares and concerns of the day flow away and focusing your mind on your connection to Sigyn.

Take a few moments to go over your day, its ups and downs, successes and failures. Quietly share that with Sigyn, lay it at Her feet, not forgetting to speak of what you're grateful for too. Offer the following prayer:

Hail to You, Sigyn, Victory Woman.
I come to You once again, Lady.
I have endured another day, sweet Mother of Sorrow.
I lay it at Your feet. Both my failures and my victories,
I give to You. You have sustained me.
You have given me the strength to persevere.
For Your gentle guidance, I give thanks,
For Your grace, and Your protection.
Please accept these humble offerings.

Light a stick of incense, a candle, and offer Her a bowl of cool water.

Sit down in front of your altar and just focus on your breathing. Take slow, deep breaths and begin to breathe in the following pattern: inhale four counts, hold four counts, exhale four counts, hold four counts. This is a basic centering breath. With each exhalation, feel the stress and tension of the day fading from you, just slipping off you like a discarded cloak. As you breathe, feel every muscle in your body release any tension. Take your time with this. I usually find that ten minutes is sufficient (set a timer if you have to, or feel you'll get antsy).

Then, change the point of your focus: as you inhale, feel yourself filled with the calm sweetness of Sigyn's strength. It is as rooted as a mountain, as cool as the ocean's tides. It does not just endure, it surmounts and stands above all obstacles. It is calm and serene. When you feel that you have meditated long enough offer up the following prayer:[10]

Sigyn, take my hand, walk with me tonight.
Above and below me let me feel Your quiet might.
Sigyn, go before, guard my right and guard my left.
Let me bask so safely in Your comfort as I rest.
Above me and below me, before me and behind
Loving Goddess, guard me, unswerving and kind.
As I now seek my rest, safe shall I be
Within Your arms so sacred, let us rest beneath the Tree.
Breath of my breath, heart of my heart

---

[10] This prayer is meant to be sung. Feel free to use it as an outline to create or adapt your own.

AN EVENING RITE TO HONOR SIGYN

Beloved Goddess Sigyn, from You may I never part.
Heart of my heart, breath of my breath
Always in Your tender arms, please allow me to rest.

    Blow out your candle or allow it to burn down.

A GROUP RITUAL TO HONOR SIGYN

By Galina Krasskova and Fuensanta Arismendi[11]

This ritual is designed to be done outdoors and there should be a sacred fire.

The Altar

An altar should be constructed with flowers and candles, an image of Sigyn if one can be found (for the past two Etinmoots, we used a fairy doll, which may sound strange but Sigyn has a strong child aspect and in that respect, it was fitting). Old fashioned keys, stones and anything else that one associates with Sigyn is also appropriate. A pretty, carved box, pretty paper and pens and diabetic stickers should also be provided at a central point on the altar. One may also include an image of Loki. Any food offerings should be laid in front of the altar on cloth. There should be a blessing bowl and a drinking horn on the altar as well and

---

[11] This rite first appeared in a slightly alternate form in *Feeding the Flame*, published in 2008 by Asphodel Press. Used with permission.

libations should be present. Something should be placed on the altar to symbolize Narvi and Vali.

Make sure everyone has a copy of the call and response.

Hallowing

Once the folk have gathered, the priest should take up a candle (or a torch if this is being done in a setting where such is appropriate) and walk deosil about the ritual space singing the Anglo Saxon *weonde* song (a song to consecrate and bless sacred space). For those unfamiliar with this chant, any appropriate means of hallowing space may be used.

The priest places the candle back on the altar and turns to welcome everyone gathered, explaining that tonight (today) we are gathered to honor the Goddess Sigyn. The priest should take the time to explain a brief bit about who Sigyn is if there are people present who are unfamiliar with this Goddess.

Invocations

At this point, three people prepared to offer invocations to Sigyn should step forward. Determine beforehand who is speaking first.

First Devotee offers her invocation standing before the altar:

"Hail to Sigyn,
Lady of the Staying Power,
Lady of Unyielding Gentleness.

A GROUP RITUAL TO HONOR SIGYN

Hail to Sigyn,
Mother of Narvi
Mother of Vali
Beloved bride of Laufey's son.

Hail to Sigyn,
Victory Maiden,
Enduring One,
Pride of Loki's Hall.

We honor You Lady this night
And ask for Your blessings.

Hail."

Devotee steps back to her place. She may light a candle, pour out a libation or offer incense before doing so, should she so desire.

Second Devotee comes before the altar. This should be a devotee who has a strong, organic connection to both Sigyn and Her children. This offering, of them all, must come from the heart.

"Beloved Sigyn,
Mother of Loss,
For Your children,
I give You my tears."

Devotee should mourn, offering her tears to Sigyn on behalf of Narvi and Vali. (I have found that to do this well takes extensive meditation before the ritual on

Sigyn's loss. It can be very difficult to enter into the necessary emotional state where this can be done with integrity. It is better to offer a written prayer rather than this visceral gift of tears if it cannot be done honestly.)

Third Devotee offers her invocation standing before the altar.

> "Because You hungered in the cave, we have brought You food.
> Because You suffered thirst, we bring You water.
> Because Your children were torn from You, we will mourn Them.
> Because Your husband is so oft maligned, we will praise Him.
> And because You, Gentle, gracious Goddess, are all too readily ignored and neglected, Your strength dismissed as naiveté, we will praise You. We will celebrate You.
> We will bring You offerings that all may know what glory rests in Loki's hall."

(I was moved when first doing this ritual to actually lay myself out face down on the floor before the altar and then move to my knees where I continued praying. I have no objection if a devotee wants to do this. I think it provides proper homage to Her and teaches those gathered the appropriate way to show respect to a God. So if the devotee is so moved, go for it. If not, don't because it should come from the heart or not at all.)

A Group Ritual to Honor Sigyn

Libations

Priest takes up the horn, filling it with alcohol, and offers it to Sigyn with the words:

> "I offer this to Sigyn, beloved Goddess, Unswerving Lady of Gentleness. May it be pleasing to You."

Then s/he pours it either into the blessing bowl or directly into the fire. The horn is filled again and poured out, this time in offering to Loki with the words:

> "I offer this to Loki, Husband of Sigyn, mad, cunning, flame-haired God of desire, God of opening. May it be pleasing to You."

Then s/he pours it either into the blessing bowl or directly into the fire. The third time, it is filled and poured out in offering to Her sons Narvi and Vali:

> "I offer this to Narvi and Vali, children of loss, children of anguish, beloved Sons of Sigyn and Loki who have been neglected, forgotten and relegated not even to the realm of memory by those who should know better. May You both be honored and may this offering be pleasing to You both. May You never be forgotten again."

Then s/he pours it either into the blessing bowl or directly into the fire.

The priest refills the horn and then passes it deosil around the gathered folk, who may drink, offering prayers to Sigyn or Her family. I like to pass the horn until the alcohol is gone and usually at least three times but gauge this by the size of the group. If it's very large, pass the horn once and pour the rest of the alcohol out in one large offering. Anything in the blessing bowl should be poured into the fire at this time as well.

Offering Box

Now the priest shows the gathered folk the carved wooden box on the altar. S/he explains that this box is to be an offering to Sigyn and will be cast into the fire before the ritual's end. Folks should be invited to come up and write prayers, requests, and/or promises on the paper provided, which can then be folded and put into Sigyn's box. Physical offerings may also be placed in the box (the one that we burned at Etinmoot had an amber necklace, a large silver ring with semi precious stones, sacred herbs, and a few other items in addition to prayers and promises written out) all with the understanding that at the end of the rite, it is all going to be consigned to flame for Sigyn. If people want to make blood offerings that is fine too. Have a sharps container handy.

The priest then invites people to sit and begins to tell Sigyn's story. There is enough material both from lore and the book *Feeding the Flame: A Devotional to Loki and His Family*, and from other personal gnosis that the storytelling can continue until everyone has had a chance to approach the box. Ideally, the storytelling should be shared out between at least two people — it makes it easier on the speaker. I like to start by asking

A GROUP RITUAL TO HONOR SIGYN

the assembled folk what they know about Sigyn and giving them time to chime in. If people have been having experiences with Her, it would be a good time to share them should they so desire. Keep an eye on the energy level and attention span of the people though and make sure this doesn't drag the energy of the ritual down. Use your judgment based on the gathered number of folk. It may be that telling Her story is enough.

Note: if the priest has meditated with Sigyn before the ritual and been given an oracle, now would be the time to read those words. If not, then telling Her story shall suffice.

Once everyone has had a chance to deal with the box, the priest should take the box to the fire and engage the folk in the following call and response:

> *Priest:* "Hail to Sigyn, Wife of Loki."
> *Response:* "Hail to Sigyn, Enduring Flame."
> *Priest:* "Hail to Sigyn, of the Staying Power."
> *Response:* "Hail to Sigyn, of quiet strength."
> *Priest:* "Hail to Sigyn, Lady of Victory."
> *Response:* "Hail to Sigyn, Mother of Loss."
> *Priest:* "Hail to Sigyn, Gentle Goddess."
> *Response:* "Hail to Sigyn, Grieving wife."
> *Priest:* "Please accept this offering Lady, with our prayers, gifts, wishes and oaths."

(The box is then placed into the bonfire.)

> *All:* "Hail, Lady Sigyn."

Closing Prayer

"We hail You, Sigyn, gracious Goddess of Loki's bower.
We hail You, Mother of loss and love and courage.
We hail You, delightful child Goddess and devastating Lady of Grief.
All that You are, we shall cherish. All that You are, we shall honor.
We shall strive, Lady, to hold Your wisdom in our hearts
in our coming in and going out, in our rising and in our resting.
May Your quiet courage, Your ceaseless forbearance inspire us.
May it humble us, as You humble us, Lady.
May we ever be open to You and to Your blessings,
Lady of the Staying Power, Beloved Sigyn.
We hail You."

This rite is ended. People may disperse or continue to pray, meditate, etc.

MEDITATION
LEARNING TO LISTEN

Because Sigyn is such a practical Goddess, She may be honored by dedicating the care of one's home and loved ones to Her. There is no fanfare in this; it is a walking, working meditation in its simplest and yet most profound form. Sigyn is a Goddess of action. It may be quiet action, it may be eminently unassuming, but it is action nonetheless. She is about doing what needs to be done to care for those dear to one's heart. She is about doing, not talking; doing, not whining or wishing or complaining or making excuses.

While meditations that focus on or even re-enact in miniature Her ordeal in the cave, or other aspects of Her story are very effective, for those not so inclined, there is a simpler way to meditate. Call Her when you're sweeping your kitchen floor. Turn the attentions of your mind and heart to Her when you're preparing dinner for your family. Reach out to Her, for Her presence and try to bring that grace into your daily, mundane life.

Sigyn may also like to be called upon in those rare moments of quiet joy: a quiet summer evening in one's garden, a morning before everyone has woken up, upon seeing a gorgeous bunch of flowers, or when you see a little child all full of chocolate ice cream hugely enjoying himself...She's not just a Goddess of action, She's a Goddess of joy too.

I believe that it's important to try to honor our Gods in as many ways as we can; to honor Sigyn not only as wife of Loki, or mother of Narvi and Vali, but as a Goddess of joy, simplicity, grace, and daring all in Her own right, for Herself as well. She is worthy of honor not for Who She is associated with, but because She simply is Herself. Sometimes it can be helpful to contemplate Who Sigyn is when She is alone, to contemplate the fullness of Her heart.

TWELVE VIRTUES OF SIGYN

by Anna Archer

Sigyn saved my life. She dragged me out of a mental and emotional darkness so deep that I thought it would devour me whole. I learned to live, love, and do something more than just survive solely by Her grace and Her hand. She restored me and because of that, I work hard every day to repay that gift; not because She asks this — She doesn't — but because it nourishes my soul to do so. She is the epitome of all things healing and good. She is deafening, thunderous, world-shattering strength; and at the same time, She is sweet, patient, gracious tenderness. I may honor many other Gods in my spiritual life, but Sigyn is my inner hearth-fire. She is the center around which everything else, all other devotion, all other work, all other being revolves.

When others ask me about my Goddess, Who She is, what She brings, what She's all about, I tell them She is a Goddess of virtue. That's an old fashioned word that, sadly, has fallen out of favor in religious discourse; but it defines Sigyn to my heart and mind perfectly. Virtue is moral excellence. A virtue is something that makes us better people. A virtue is something one should strive to develop and nourish. Their seeds may rest nascent in our souls but it takes work to make those seeds blossom. It's like fanning tendrils of smoke into a roaring flame when making a campfire, and then conscientiously tending that fire so that it does not die out. Being virtuous doesn't just happen; it is a goal that one has to work toward, fumbling all the way. That's one of the things that Sigyn taught me: virtue isn't a thing so much as commitment to a way of being in the world, a way of interacting with others, a way of developing the self, a path upon which one has chosen to walk. It's nodding one's head to one's failures and then getting up, dusting oneself off, and getting back to work yet again. Virtue is about not giving up on the development and care of the soul.

When I pray and meditate throughout my day on my Lady, I often find myself returning again and again to twelve specific virtues. These are the aspects of Her nature that most stand out for me, that I find most useful in my own life and work, to meditate upon. Like many Sigyn's women that I've talked to, I get very tired of hearing my Goddess dismissed as naïve, deceived, abused, downtrodden, or any of the thousand dismissive terms that are used by so many in the Asatru community to ignore and disregard Her. Is it so difficult to comprehend that She made a choice of the heart and everything else about Her story was simply part and parcel of standing firmly by that choice? She may be unwavering in Her devotion but that is because She chooses to be and disciplines Her heart in this manner.

It is not blindness. It is not stupidity. It is not weakness. It is a choice. She is in total control of Her destiny.

The virtues that I most often find myself returning to again and again with Sigyn, the things that mark the internal altar of my devotions to Her are simple:

Strength: Strength isn't just about being physically strong. That is its least manifestation. Strength is about not allowing oneself to be broken by circumstance; it's about holding true to one's word and one's devotion even when it brings great pain. I don't think there can be virtue without the development of inner strength. Without some measure of strength, one folds at the first challenge. Sigyn is like the mountain, or like steel in her heart. She does not bend in Her commitments. She does not swerve from the path She has chosen to walk. She does what She has decided to do, and that is enough.

Loyalty: From Her strength flows Her loyalty. She remains committed and constant. I often call Her My Lady of the Constant Heart or My Lady of Constancy. She doesn't take the easy way out. She doesn't betray or abandon Her family when everyone else turns against Them. She maintains both Her dignity and Her commitment to both Her husband and children. I know that for me, there are so many lessons in this part of Her story. It's easy to be swayed from a decision or a commitment or a path when it seems like every single hand is raised against you. It's easy to back down, or to not speak up, or to allow the discord of others to shake one's determination. I look to Sigyn to preserve me from moral cowardice. I look to Her to preserve me from the insidious creeping rot of taking the easy way out and the habits it breeds.

Graciousness: This is a corollary of Her strength and the totality of all the other virtues that I might speak about here. This is where Her greatness comes from. It is elegance of the heart. Grace comes from all the other virtues that She possesses: Her strength isn't aggression, Her strength is resilience; Her loyalty isn't blind (She knows well Her husband's faults), it is deliberately constant. She is as graceful as the North Star and as unwavering. She doesn't waste time on being offended. Nor does She dignity adverse events by railing against them. She gets on with what needs to be done.

Humility: Sigyn doesn't boast. She allows Her work and accomplishments to speak for themselves. If one cannot see that She is worthy of honor, then that speaks far more about the person than it does about the Goddess in question. There's no false pride with my Lady. She teaches quiet, well-earned pride in one's work well done, but there's no need to boast or jostle for attention, or create disruption and jealousy, enmity, and irritation by constantly, publicly stealing the spotlight. She has better things to do. Her character is mature enough, strong enough not to need the constant rush of external validation to make one feel worthy. She knows She has worth. I have often observed that those who boast endlessly about who they are and what they do seldom accomplish half as much as those who avoid public displays of pride instead preferring to allow the incontrovertible voice of their work to speak on their behalf. Sigyn is like that: She is about doing what is right and what needs to be done; not what will win Her awards or praise from others. In this, Her integrity lies.

Gentleness: She is amazingly strong and unyielding, and sometimes even firm and implacable but She is always gentle. It isn't that She couldn't be violent and harsh; it's that She chooses not to be. She is just as powerful as any other Goddess. She has Her passions, Her desires, Her needs, Her angers, Her wants, Her hurts. With an incredibly disciplined will, a remarkable self-discipline, She chooses how She is going to express Herself. She decides very consciously how She will leave Her mark on those around Her, and Her choice is gentleness. It's something that She chooses every minute of every day not because She is weak or afraid, but because the alternative would diminish Her soul. Maybe I should refer to Her as a Goddess of self-discipline, because that is surely one of Her strongest characteristics: I pray it is not hubris to say that Her will puts the other Gods to shame.

Charity: Charity is hospitality in action. We Asatruar talk a lot about the importance of 'hospitality' but often fail to live up to our words. The power of this virtue resides in the will: one chooses to act with loving-kindness, one chooses to act in a welcoming, gracious manner, one chooses courtesy over discord even in the face of one's enemies. It is not about the other person. It is about doing that which does not diminish the self. Sigyn is strong enough not to find the expression of charity a threat to Her own power. Charity may be as simple as biting back hostile words; it may call for one to put one's exhaustion to the side and greeting the newcomer with warm words of welcome, it may mean standing up in defense of someone being unjustly slandered, it may mean offering half a sandwich to a co-worker having a bad day. There are a thousand little ways in which charity is an option, if we choose to take it. That has been Her challenge to me, almost on a daily basis: am I secure enough in myself as a human being, as Her devotee, as *me* not to fear extending the blessing of charity to those around me? Sometimes, to my dismay, the answer is no but I'm working on it.

Fidelity: Fidelity is more than loyalty; it implies faithful, careful attention to one's duties. It implies a fealty to the highest aspects of one's soul, one's own highest good. It is the umbrella under which all the other virtues may blossom. Fidelity, that care and mindful attention to everything for which one is responsible, to everything to which one has committed is the hallmark of all that Sigyn teaches. This is the hidden virtue, the one that is never spoken about, but that makes all the others possible. Fidelity isn't glamorous. It's quiet. It's unassuming. It's essential. It is the building block of constancy, the mortar of devotion. I give my fidelity to Sigyn: I give Her the absolute allegiance of my heart.

TWELVE VIRTUES OF SIGYN

Love: Oh, this is the fire that makes all other things, all other hardships, all other sacrifices possible. This is the bond, the connection, the rushing river of committed will underlying every one of Her actions. This is why She chooses constancy, gentleness, and devotion. If Sigyn is my North Star, love is Her North Star. What else can be written about love? With Sigyn, it is all-encompassing.

Endurance: When I was in college, I studied the Japanese language for several years. The symbol, or *kanji*, for 'endurance' is the *kanji* for 'sword' poised over the *kanji* for 'heart.' That defines this virtue for me when I think about Sigyn: that sword may move, it may plunge into the heart beneath it, but that heart will not move. Its beating may stop, but it's purpose will not be thwarted. It will hold; its power will hold; its purpose will hold; it will hold true to its purpose. It is the proud declaration (to paraphrase Luther) of "Here I stand, I cannot do otherwise." It is a firmness of conviction and commitment that brooks no compromise and perseveres in the face of every challenge. That is the essence of Sigyn's heart, to me. It is my goal for how I want my own heart to be for Her. When I contemplate the immense courage that such conviction, such endurance demands, it makes me cry, it tears open my heart, it shows me Sigyn in Her glory and greatness.

Patience: For all Her strength, Sigyn, more than any other God or Goddess that I have ever loved, seldom feels the need to rush anything. As She is gentle, as She endures, so is She patient. She allows things to unfold in the time of their own becoming without feeling the need to interfere in every little thing. There is nothing impetuous about my Lady. Instead, there is a steadfastness, a stillness, an endless patience that is grounded in the fidelity and love that make up so great a part of Her nature. She does not feel the need to dominate or control because She Herself is secure in Her position, Her power, Herself. She knows that She can meet anything that might come Her way rightly. I envy this almost more than anything else about Her. I am not patient. I fret, I am anxious, I push and twist and pull at the bindings of my life when She instead would have me observe, embrace, and work within them toward personal greatness. She takes that which is ordinary, that which is unremarkable and through ongoing care and patient attention transforms it into burnished gold. I have placed my heart and soul in Her hands with the prayer that She might do the same to me. She stays the course.

Simplicity: Sigyn doesn't clutter things up by excess baggage, or ornamentation, or decoration, or fancy words. She just does what needs to be done cleanly, without flashiness, without drama. It is this, almost more than any other virtue that makes me feel like I can just breathe a great, huge sigh of relief and sink into Her arms like a child with its mother. Clutter distracts. Sigyn is not about distraction. A commitment to simplicity allows the bold truth of a matter to shine through, unimpeded by fancy words, or gestures, by drama or hyperbole. Plain action, quiet words: these things allow room for a deed to stand on its own merits. These things allow room for truth and integrity to grow.

Mindfulness: I have a friend who defines 'mindfulness' as the Zen of being in the moment. I don't much have this gift. I tend to be accident-prone because I am always rushing to get to the next thing that must be done instead of giving my full attention to what I am doing at any given moment. Sigyn has much to teach me about mindfulness and I think that maybe I left this virtue to the end of my list because it is such a difficult one for me to even approach. Mindfulness flows from patient care and attention, from honoring the sacred in those ordinary tasks that must be done again and again, day after day, week after week, month after month, year after year. Mindfulness means slowing down and breathing and realizing that all that is sacred or holy isn't 'out there' somewhere, but here, in the moment, in what we do, each little thing, in our day to day lives and interactions. That, for me at least, is a terrifying thought. It's also honoring the time it takes to do something, or cook something, or go somewhere: not wanting to rush it into the next part of the process, but honoring the time things take. Sigyn is about giving every moment its value, its integrity, its honor, its due. A given moment will never come again. It is a gift lost forever. To honor the moment, is to honor the task, both what is being done, those that are doing, and the time that it takes to do. That is one of Sigyn's most difficult lessons: just being in the moment and mindful, without wanting to be anywhere else.

I have found my way to these virtues and through them, to Sigyn. If this article helps others come to know Her a little bit better than that is good too. These are my touchstones, the things that I return to again and again in my devotion to Her. They are guideposts on what for me, has been a long and difficult journey. In the end, I want my whole life to be a song of praise to Her. She has given me so very much, it is the least that I can give in return.

A MEDITATION ON SIGYN'S BOWL

by Fuensanta Arismendi

I am burned beyond words.
Deeds are hollow.
My soul is as light as a fossil
beyond all passion, all joy, all love.
But love spawned duty once and for love's dead sake,
I'll hold the bowl,
go through the motions,
and hope they taste to You
as once loved ones did.
Please may this be as cruel and brief
as the ebbing tide;
and may the blessed waves
wash us clean of this drought.
I'll hold the bowl.

We tend to think of Sigyn holding the bowl in a continual state of love. That is a simplistic view and it diminishes Her image. Her unyielding gentleness, Her invincible strength, comes from this: that She holds the bowl when She loves Loki and when She is angry at

Him, and when She is too weary for love or anger or any other emotion. She holds the bowl when She knows why She is holding it and She holds the bowl when pain erases all memory of why She is holding it. She is as unwavering as the North Star.

This meditation evolved as a consequence of putting out food and wine in offering to Loki and Sigyn every night, together with two small towels, one dry, one damp to feed and wash that part of Them that might still be in the cave. One day it occurred to me to hold the bowl for Sigyn for ten minutes, so They could have some small moment of peace as They ate. I have been doing this nightly ever since.

Hold the bowl. I never thought it would feel so foreign and yet so right to do so. We always think of serving the Gods by scurrying around doing things. Now I serve by 'just standing there.' I serve just by keeping still. My back itches. *Hold the bowl.* What does She have to look at as She holds the bowl day after day, year after year? Is Her Husband all She looks at, all She needs? Or does She sometimes look away, to dank walls and bare ground? Can She see Loki at all, or is it dark in the cave, endless night? *Hold the bowl.* If it is dark, how can She tell when the bowl overflows? When Loki screams? Damn, I'm crying and I can't blow my nose. *Hold the bowl.* Do They speak to each other? What is there to articulate when this endless choice to stay and endure says all that needs to be said? Does Sigyn think of Her children or has grief turned Her to stone, the better to give Her strength? No, I don't think so — She is the Lady of the Invincible Heart, the

A MEDITATION ON SIGYN'S BOWL

Goddess of Unyielding Gentleness. *Hold the bowl.* Time is going so slowly and I know I'll stop after ten minutes — what must it feel like for Her, who does not even know if this will ever stop, this infinity of stillness and grief and pain? *Hold the bowl.*

The monologue goes on, combining fervor and triviality. At times, one reaches a state of grace in which no thoughts or feelings intrude. All one's being is intent on simply being still, and being there. And when the ten minutes have elapsed, part of me is relieved to stop, and part of me feels exiled from my true place, the place I fear, the place I pray to be in because if They are in that cave, then that cave is my only home. *Hold the bowl.*

I keep a special bowl that I have dedicated to Sigyn for just this purpose and I use it for nothing else. It does collect poison and needs to be cleaned very carefully after each time because of that. Ten minutes seems like nothing until the weight of the bowl fills my hands, pulls at my arms. It seems to me that if everyone who loved Sigyn and Loki held the bowl for just a little bit, just ten minutes a day perhaps, She would not have to hold it at all.

IN PRAISE OF SIGYN

You are unyielding
You will not be moved.
Let others rant and rave and curse.
Where love has rooted itself in Your heart
even the might of the mountain is weak.

You are fierce: a she wolf defending Her own.
No one expects it of You, Sweet Sigyn.
Because You do not wear Your might
as others might wear gleaming jewels,
no one thinks You strong,
a force with which to reckon.

Yours however is the power
that grants no acknowledgment
to that which would turn You from Your course.
You are His North Star, forever constant,
a gleaming beacon, His only comfort
a whisper of half forgotten joy
in the abyssal eternity of the cave.

Your eyes are on Your task,
Asgard truly should fear,

and then pour out offerings
to whatever Powers the Powers honor
lest You turn Your heart to justified vengeance,
on the day You and Your Husband
rise from the pit.

Vengeance is rarely Your way, however,
it is often too great a luxury to nurture in Your heart
in light of the work You must do.
Some sacrifices after all must be made
and You are pragmatic.
Vengeance will not return a murdered son.
Vengeance will not remake a shattered God.
Your way is simply to endure,
which is not so simple at all;
to endure and hold in Your burning heart
the knowledge that nothing lasts forever.
There is only the wyrd woven
strand by black and bloody strand,
in the crucible of necessary choice.
There is only a strength beyond courage
and the heart and character of valor
plucked from amidst the weaving.

To You, Lady, I bow my head.
Lady of Enduring Grace,
Lady of Valor,
Lady of Victory.

SIGYN: WOMAN OF VALOR

A woman of valor,
who can find?
Her value is greater
than any duergar-made jewel.

She enriches Her husband's hall.
She is the sanctuary of His heart.

She strengthens and supports Him all his days.
With Her at His side, He shall lack in nothing.

She is the guardian of Their hearth.
Her hands are industrious,
Her heart is willing.
She fills Her home with delight.

She does not tarry in idleness,
but nourishes all who are within Her care.
She is diligent at the spindle,
and keeps the keys of Her Husband's hall.
She maintains a fruitful, frithful home
and Her heart is ever strong.

Those under Her care have nothing to fear.
She sets Her hands to the distaff,
She holds the spindle in her palms.
She clothes and feeds Her household
and Their pantry is never bare.

She is courageous,
Strength and honor are Her clothing,
She meets the future with courage.
Her lips bestow wisdom,
and Her tongue is ever kind.
Constancy is Her brightest jewel.

Her children praise Her.
Her husband adores Her.
She surpasses all women in honor.
Her piety is Her shield.
Her sweetness of heart Her strength.

All temporal beauty fades,
but the mighty heart
of a valorous woman is forever.
Let Her home be full of abundance,
She adorned with every blessing.

Always, Her works will praise Her.

FIVE FOR SIGYN

We praise You, Lady of Constancy,
Whose heart never wavers in Her devotion.
We praise You, Victory Woman,
Whose strength is that of unending endurance.
We praise You, North Star,
Whose virtue will never be diminished.
We praise You, Wife of Loki,
beloved Jewel of His hall, cherished beyond measure.
We praise You, Incantation Fetter,
Whose touch brings healing and liberation.
We praise You, Mother of Two clever Sons, loss and
glory and love everlasting.

Oh, Lady Strong as the Mountain!
Oh, Love Longer Lasting than the Stars!
Oh, Sweet and Ferocious Devotion!
Oh, Never-swerving Power!
Oh, Heart of Loki's Hall!
Ever and always shall You be praised, Sigyn.

INCANTATION FETTER

She is called Incantation Fetter.
She holds in Her heart
the power of making
and of unmaking
those things that matter.

What other Gods have done,
She has the power to undo.
What other Gods have set in motion,
She holds the power to stop.
Her heart is valor and victory.

She is called Incantation Fetter.
This does not mean Her gifts
are borne without some price.
She stops the venom from searing Her mate
through the shield of Her own body.

She stops Her husband's torture
from destroying any vestige of mind and heart,
through sharing His dark imprisonment.
All power has a price.
All gifts demand certain sacrifices.

That is why they are not to be born lightly.
Sigyn holds Her world together.
No one ever mentions the cost
such careful, stubborn knitting takes on Her.
She is called Incantation Fetter, praise Her.

                Great love is service.
                                  - Daphne Kingma

LITANY FOR SIGYN

Sigyn, Light in the Cave
Sigyn, Mother of Mourning
Sigyn, Lady of Comfort
Sigyn, Victory Woman
Sigyn, Northern Star
Sigyn, Loki's Sanctuary
Sigyn, Indomitable Goddess
Sigyn, Holder of the Bowl
Sigyn, Goddess of Anguish
Sigyn, Who unbinds all fetters
Sigyn, delight of Her husband
Sigyn, Who does not yield
Sigyn, strength of the mountain
Sigyn, playful child
Sigyn, Lady of Joy
Sigyn, Lady of Unyielding Gentleness
Sigyn, Lady of Constancy
Sigyn, Lady of the Staying Power
Teach us the way of devotion.

EPILOGUE

Truth is a journey toward magnificence.
— Daphne Kingma

This book has been a labor of love for a Goddess who in many ways has transformed my life. Though I belong to Odin, the fine thread of Sigyn's gentle presence has, for many years, wound its way unerringly through the twisting, rough-hewn halls of my heart. She has been my haven, when the demands of my own Lord have sometimes grown too hard to bear; and She has taught me how to call upon the love and devotion in my own heart, to find the strength to take up my work once more. She has sustained me and for that, I shall always be grateful. More than that, though, She has sustained those that I dearly love. My adopted mother belongs in part to Sigyn and this book is as much a gift to her as it is to the Goddess she adores above all others.

It has been an immense privilege to know a handful of Sigyn's women and devotees throughout my life and like the Goddess they serve, their human example has been one of inspiration. I'd like to acknowledge those writers and poets who contributed articles and prayers to this book (whether I chose to use them or not — I received far more submissions than I was able to include, given the narrow scope of this work). Thank you for your heartfelt contributions.

In the end, when the question of how to honor the Gods is raised what more can I say than this: just do it. The act of doing will teach you what needs to be done. The act of doing will transform your life.

SUGGESTIONS FOR FURTHER READING

Arismendi, Fuensanta, and Krasskova, Galina (2008). *Root, Stone, and Bone*. MA: Asphodel Press.

Barks, Coleman, (2003). *Rumi: The Book of Love*. NY: Harper Collins Publishers.

Barrows, Anita and Macy, Joanna, (2005). *Rilke's Book of Hours: Love Poems to God*. NY: Riverhead Books.

Gyll, Andrew, (2009). *Shadow Gods and Black Fire*. MA: Asphodel Press.

Hirshfield, Jane, (1994). *Women in Praise of the Sacred*. NY: Harper Perennial.

Kaldera, Raven, (2006). *Jotunbok: Working with the Giants of the Northern Tradition*. MA: Asphodel Press.

Kaldera, Raven, (2006). *The Pathwalker's Guide to the Nine Worlds*. MA: Asphodel Press.

Kaldera, Raven and Galina Krasskova, (2009). *Northern Tradition for the Solitary Practitioner*. NJ: New Page Books.

Kingma, Daphne Rose, (1998). *The Future of Love*. NY: Doubleday.

Krasskova, Galina, (2019). *A Modern Guide to Heathenry*. Newburyport, MA: Red Wheel/Weiser.

Krasskova, Galina, (2008). *Feeding the Flame: A Devotional to Loki and His Family*. MA: Asphodel Press.

Maestas, Silence, (2008). *Walking the Heart Road*. MA: Asphodel Press.

Nichols, Tracy, (2009). *Love Songs for Laufey's Son*. MA: Asphodel Press.

Nichols, Tracy, (2007). *From the Heart, For the Heart*. MA: Asphodel Press.

Therese of Lisieux, (1996). *The Story of a Soul: The Autobiography of St. Therese of Lisieux*. Washington, D.C.: ICS Publications. (*I realize this is a Christian text but Therese's "little way" is so quintessentially Sigyn-ish, that I strongly feel this book will be valuable for those wishing to honor Sigyn*).

Vongvisith, Elizabeth, (2006). *Trickster, My Beloved: Poems for Laufey's Son*. MA: Asphodel Press.

Vongvisith, Elizabeth, (2009). *Be Thou My Heart and Shield*. MA: Asphodel Press.

ABOUT THE AUTHOR

Galina Krasskova is a Heathen priest and vitki with over two decades of practice. She is also the author of over thirty books on Heathenry, devotion, and polytheism including *He is Frenzy: Collected Writings on Odin* and *A Modern Guide to Heathenry*. She holds a Masters in Religious Studies (2009), a Masters in Medieval Studies (2019) and is currently pursuing a PhD in Theology. She maintains an active blog at krasskova.wordpress.com.

> Those who profess to favor freedom, yet deprecate agitation, are men who want crops without planting up the ground. They want the rain without thunder or lightning. They want the ocean without the awful roar of its many waters. The struggle may be a moral one; or it may be a physical one; or it may be both moral and physical; but it must be a struggle. Power concedes nothing without a demand. It never did and it never will.
> - Frederick Douglas

Made in United States
Troutdale, OR
12/22/2023